Chumash

F.A. BIRD

An Imprint of Abdo Publishing
abdobooks.com

ABDOBOOKS.COM

Published by Abdo Publishing, a division of ABDO, PO Box 398166, Minneapolis, Minnesota 55439.

Printed in the United States of America, North Mankato, Minnesota
102024
012025

Editor: Lauri Nelson
Design: Mighty Media, Inc.

Cover Photograph: Eyal Nahmias/Alamy Stock Photo
Interior Photographs: Ad_hominem/Shutterstock Images, p. 7; Angel Wynn/NativeStock, pp. 11, 19, 27; Citizen of the Planet/UCG/Universal Images Group/Getty Images, p. 5; HannaTor/Shutterstock Images, p. 23; Nature and Science/Alamy Stock Photo, p. 25; Nik Wheeler/Corbis/Getty Images, p. 15; PJ Heller/ZUMAPRESS.com/Alamy Stock Photo, p. 29; Ralph T. Coe Collection, Gift of Ralph T. Coe Foundation for the Arts, 2011/The MET, p. 17; Salameh dibaei/Getty Images, p. 13; Spencer Weiner/Los Angeles Times/Getty Images, p. 21; Universal Images Group/Getty Images, p. 9

Library of Congress Control Number: 2024938797

Publisher's Cataloging-in-Publication Data
Names: Bird, F.A., author.
Title: Chumash / by F.A. Bird
Description: Minneapolis, Minnesota : ABDO Publishing, 2025 | Series: Native American nations | Includes online resources and index.
Identifiers: ISBN 9781098296216 (lib. bdg.) | ISBN 9798384917328 (ebook)
Subjects: LCSH: Chumash Indians--Juvenile literature. | Native Americans--Juvenile literature. | Indians of North America--Juvenile literature. | Indigenous peoples--Social life and customs--Juvenile literature. | Cultural anthropology--Juvenile literature.
Classification: DDC 973.0497--dc23

Contents

Homelands

Chumash (CHOO-mash) homelands are located in what is now California. Their territory once included parts of present-day southern California and the Channel Islands. The Chumash lived along the coast, on islands, and inland.

The Coastal Chumash lived along the shores of the Pacific Ocean. Their land had beaches, dunes, and **estuaries**. Shrubs, willow trees, and **tule** (TOO-lee) grew on their land.

The Island Chumash homelands were on islands in the Pacific Ocean. They lived on the Santa Cruz, Santa Rosa, San Miguel, and Anacapa Islands. These islands were home to many plants and animals.

The Inland Chumash lived near mountains, rivers, and oak trees. The territory bordered the San Joaquin (san-wah-KEEN) Valley and the western coast of California. This territory included Mount Pinos, near present-day Santa Barbara. The Chumash considered Mount Pinos sacred.

Morro Rock in Morro Bay, California, is sacred to the Chumash.

Society

Chumash society was tiered. At the top of the society were the medicine people and astrologers. Astrologers helped guide the Chumash by carefully watching and charting the stars.

Chiefs called *wot* ranked just below the medicine people and astrologers. A man or a woman could inherit the title of chief. A chief had many duties. These duties included feeding the poor, protecting the people, and arranging hunting and gathering trips. Ceremonial leaders and messengers helped the chiefs with these duties.

The skilled artisans were below the chiefs. The artisans made items such as beads, which were used for trade and decoration. Below the skilled artisans were the laborers. The poor class was at the bottom.

The Chumash spoke about eight related languages. These were from the Hokan language family. Each Chumashan language had its own unique sound system.

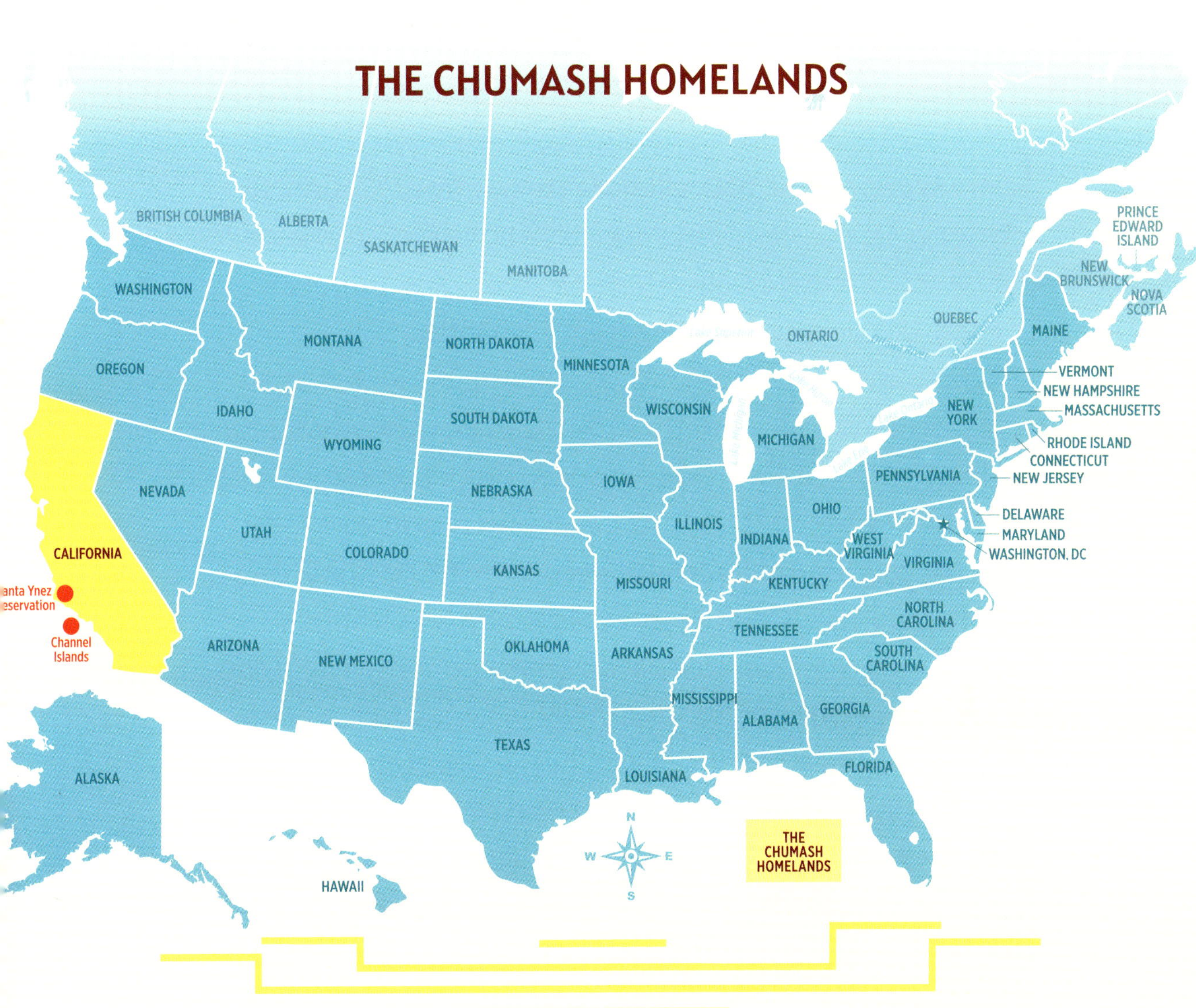

THE CHUMASH HOMELANDS
BRITISH COLUMBIA
ALBERTA
SASKATCHEWAN
MANITOBA
ONTARIO
QUEBEC
PRINCE EDWARD ISLAND
NEW BRUNSWICK
NOVA SCOTIA
WASHINGTON
OREGON
CALIFORNIA
anta Ynez
eservation
Channel Islands
IDAHO
NEVADA
MONTANA
WYOMING
UTAH
ARIZONA
COLORADO
NEW MEXICO
NORTH DAKOTA
SOUTH DAKOTA
NEBRASKA
KANSAS
OKLAHOMA
TEXAS
MINNESOTA
IOWA
MISSOURI
ARKANSAS
LOUISIANA
WISCONSIN
ILLINOIS
MICHIGAN
INDIANA
OHIO
KENTUCKY
TENNESSEE
MISSISSIPPI
ALABAMA
GEORGIA
FLORIDA
SOUTH CAROLINA
NORTH CAROLINA
VIRGINIA
WEST VIRGINIA
PENNSYLVANIA
NEW YORK
MAINE
VERMONT
NEW HAMPSHIRE
MASSACHUSETTS
RHODE ISLAND
CONNECTICUT
NEW JERSEY
DELAWARE
MARYLAND
WASHINGTON, DC
ALASKA
HAWAII
N
W
E
S
THE CHUMASH HOMELANDS

Homes

There were about 100 villages throughout Chumash territory. The settlements consisted of extended families that lived in homes called *'aps* (AHPS). The homes were shaped like domes and covered in thatch.

The frame of a Chumash *'ap* was made with willow poles. To build a frame, the Chumash put the ends of sapling willow poles in the ground. They bent the poles at the top to meet in the center, forming a dome.

Next, the Chumash tied on cross poles with **cordage** made from milkweed fibers. This made the frame sturdy. Sometimes, the Chumash used whalebone to make the frame even stronger.

The Chumash covered their homes with thatch mats. They made the mats from **tule**, bulrush, or cattail stalks. They tied the mats onto the frame, leaving a hole at the top to let smoke out and light in. They could close the hole with a cover made of animal skin.

'Aps were built in different sizes. One could house as few as four people or as many as 50.

Food

The Chumash hunted, fished, and gathered their food. Inland, they used bows and arrows to hunt large prey. The Chumash also hunted rabbits, quails, ducks, and songbirds. They caught these animals in traps, snares, and nets.

Along the shore and on the islands, the Chumash hunted sea mammals with **harpoons**. These animals included seals, otters, pilot whales, and porpoises.

The men fished using basket traps. The traps let fish swim into a wide, open end, and led to a narrow, closed end that stopped fish from escaping. The Chumash also used a hook and line to fish. They made hooks from **abalone** shells and lines from twisted plant fibers.

The Chumash women gathered berries, cherries, wild plants, seeds, cattails, pine nuts, and acorns. Acorns were a staple food for the Chumash. They roasted the acorns and ground them into flour. Then, they made the flour into mush and cakes.

The Chumash cooked ground acorns with water to make a soup or stew.

CHAPTER 5

Clothing

In warm weather, the Chumash did not wear much clothing. When they did wear clothing, it was made of woven bird feathers, animal skins, and plant fibers. In the winter, the Chumash wore capes made from animal hides, woven rabbit skins, and plant fibers.

Men wore nets around their waist. They used the nets like pockets to carry water jugs and other items. The nets were made of **cordage** woven from milkweed fibers and bird **down**. Woodpecker, magpie, gull, and hawk feathers were attached to the netting.

Chumash women wore cordage skirts. They also wore dresses. Women made their dresses by sewing together patches of rabbit or bird skins. They decorated their clothing with shells.

Both men and women often wore sandals and painted their bodies. To make the paint, they mixed milkweed sap with colored minerals. Each village had its own design.

Feathers, cordage, and shells are worn at the Malibu Chumash Day Powwow and Intertribal Celebration.

Crafts

The Chumash had many artistic skills. Chumash men made beads from **olivella** shells. These beads were valuable and used as money. The Chumash were also excellent basket makers. They decorated their baskets with **geometric** designs using dyes made from plants.

The Chumash made three types of baskets. Coil baskets could hold liquids. These baskets were woven with bulrush and willow. Then the Chumash put hot rocks and crushed asphalt into the baskets. As the hot rocks melted the asphalt, the baskets became waterproof.

Twine baskets could be used for gathering and storing seeds, meal, and water. The Chumash used twine to make seed beater baskets. The seed beater knocked seeds off grasses into a gathering basket.

Coarsely woven baskets had many uses, too. Some people used these baskets as strainers. The Chumash also used these baskets as traps to catch fish.

Chumash baskets take a long time to make. The women must gather, dry, split, dye, trim, and soak the plants before starting to weave.

Family

The men, women, and elders in Chumash families had different responsibilities. Women gathered food and cooked. They used digging sticks to unearth roots and bulbs that could be safely eaten. Men made tools and other items. The elders helped raise the family.

Chumash women also worked with steatite, a type of stone. They cooked in steatite ollas, which are containers used for cooking and storage. They baked on flat cooking stones. The men of a Chumash family also worked with steatite. They carved beads, bowls, and charms from steatite.

Men were also responsible for making tomol canoes from redwood. They drilled and lashed redwood planks together. Then they sealed the seams and drill holes with asphalt. The asphalt made the plank canoes waterproof. If they got a splinter while working, the Chumash would remove it with clamshell tweezers.

Steatite canoe with shell decorations. Steatite is softer than most stones. People call it "soapstone" because it feels like soap.

Children

The Chumash carried their babies on basketry cradleboards. The Chumash wove their cradleboards from **tule** or willow.

As the children grew, they learned by watching and helping the adults. For example, Chumash girls learned how to make baskets. They learned how to prepare rabbit skins and weave them into blankets. They also learned how to strip milkweed plants for **cordage**.

Chumash boys learned how to hunt and fish. They learned how to craft the tools they needed, such as fishing traps. They also made **sinew**-backed bows and bird-**down** arrows.

Chumash children often watched as artisans made beads and bird-bone hairpins. The children also had time to run, swim, and play games. For example, they played a game of dice with walnut shells filled with asphalt. They judged their points by how the dice landed.

The Chumash decorated their walnut shell game pieces with broken pieces of abalone shells.

Traditions

The Chumash have a myth about how their people were created. A long time ago, the earth was very quiet. Earth Mother, Hutash, decided to make humans. Humans could fill the earth with beautiful sounds.

Hutash created the Chumash from magic seeds and placed them on an island. It was in the Pacific Ocean near present-day Santa Barbara. Sky Snake, Hutash's husband, sent a bolt of lightning. This brought fire to the Chumash.

Soon, the Island Chumash became very noisy. Hutash was getting a headache from all the noise. She decided the time had come to move some of the people. She created a rainbow bridge from the island to the mainland.

Some Chumash crossed the bridge. They found the coast and the inland to be beautiful and full of wonderful foods. But along the way, some of the people fell off the bridge. Hutash did not want her people to drown. So, she turned the fallen people into dolphins.

The Chumash people honor Hutash every year with a fall harvest festival named after her.

CHAPTER 10

War

The Chumash were a peaceful and friendly people. They usually got along with their neighboring tribes. So, they did not go to war often.

It was the chief's job to get permission for hunting, fishing, and gathering in other communities. If the other community did not agree, a war would break out.

When the Chumash went to war, they used bows and arrows. For close combat, they fought with knives made from flint or shell. Men carried small knives in their hair.

The Chumash were organized in battle. First, they sent a messenger to their enemy. The messenger arranged the time when the battle would happen.

At the set time, the Chumash met the other group. They threw feathers into the air and shouted war cries. One side shot a series of arrows at the other side. Then, the other side shot the same number of arrows. After each side shot its arrows, the conflict ended.

A war shield protects the wearer from arrows and clubs. It is also worn during traditional dances.

Contact with Europeans

The Chumash were the first major California tribe to meet Europeans. A brief meeting took place with Portuguese explorer Juan Rodríguez Cabrillo in 1542. Also, in 1602, Spanish explorer Sebastián Vizcaíno met the Chumash. He arrived on the feast day of Saint Barbara. So, his landing spot was named Santa Barbara.

The Chumash were friendly to the Europeans. In the 1700s, the Spaniards, with help from some of the Chumash, built Roman Catholic **missions** on Chumash lands. Many Chumash joined the missionary system.

Learning the ways of the missions caused many Chumash to lose their languages and traditions. Many Chumash also died from sicknesses the Europeans had brought with them. The Chumash had no **immunity** to illnesses such as **smallpox** or the common cold.

Juan Bautista de Anza was another Spanish explorer. He wrote journals that included his meeting with the Chumash in 1776.

CHAPTER 12

Chumash Leaders

The Chumash had many leaders over the years. Some tried to prevent the Spaniards from converting the people to Christianity. Others thought conversion was good.

One Chumash leader who converted to Christianity was Chief Pedro Yanonali. He helped the Spaniards when they were setting up **missions** in the area. Over time, other Chumash also converted to Christianity. Leaders today believe this put the Chumash way of life in danger.

Today, leaders are working hard to protect the Chumash **culture**. Mati Waiya, or Little Hawk, is one such person. He is a Chumash ceremonial leader. He conducts ceremonies such as the solstice ceremony.

Waiya also teaches schoolchildren about Chumash culture. He has worked with others to create a museum called Wishtoyo's Chumash Village. At the village, people can see how the Chumash once lived. Waiya is also working to protect Chumash cultural and historic sites.

Chumash elder Beverly Folkes works with others to preserve their culture, customs, and traditions for younger generations.

The Chumash Today

Today the Chumash live worldwide. Some live within their original lands. Many have become doctors, lawyers, and teachers. About 5,000 people say they have Chumash ancestors.

Over the years, the Chumash lost a lot of land. Their homelands once covered about 7,000 square miles (18,130 sq km). Today, many Chumash groups have no land base. These Chumash are seeking lands, and they hope to become **federally recognized**.

The Santa Ynez Band of Chumash is the only federally recognized band of Chumash. The reservation has 1,500 acres (607 ha) of land, near Santa Barbara, California. This includes a new Chumash Museum and Cultural Center.

The Chumash still gather and hold ceremonies. The children are learning the stories and history of their people. The Chumash are working hard to protect their **culture** and environment, and to live in peace.

The annual Intertribal Powwow in Santa Ynez, California, brings over 300 singers and dancers together to honor and celebrate their ancestors.

Glossary

abalone—edible, spineless animals that cling to rocks.

cordage—ropes or cords made by twisting plant fibers.

cradleboard—a flat board used to hold a baby. It could be carried on the mother's back or hung from a tree so that the baby could see what was going on.

culture—the customs, arts, and tools of a nation or people at a certain time.

down—soft, fluffy feathers.

estuary—the body of water where a river's current meets an ocean's tide.

federal recognition—the US government's recognition of a tribe as being an independent nation. The tribe is eligible for special funding and protection of its lands.

geometric—made up of straight lines, circles, and other simple shapes.

harpoon—a spear used to kill seals, walruses, and whales.

immunity—protection against disease.

mission—a center or headquarters for religious work.

olivella—a beach animal with a shell and no backbone.

sinew—a band of tough fibers that joins a muscle to a bone.

smallpox—a disease that can cause fever and skin irritations that leave blisters.

tiered—organized in such a way that some people are above others.

tule—a type of reed that grows in wetlands. Tule is native to California.

ONLINE RESOURCES

To learn more about the Chumash, please visit **abdobooklinks.com** or scan this QR code. These links are routinely monitored and updated to provide the most current information available.

Index